8 Things to Break Up With After Your Breakup

How to heal and release the energy from old relationships to make room for new beginnings

Maiya Katherine

Copyright © 2024 by Blue Dragonfly Life ™

All rights reserved. Published in the United States of America. No part of this book may be reproduced or transmitted in any form or by any means, graphic, electronic or mechanical, including photocopying, recording, taping or by any information storage or retrieval system, without permission in writing from the publisher.

This edition published by Blue Dragonfly Life™
Produced for BDL by Highpoint Executive Publishing.
For information, write to info@bluedragonflylife.com.
First Edition
ISBN: 979-8-9897773-8-9

Library of Congress Cataloging-in-Publication Data
Katherine, Maiya
8 Things to Break Up With After Your Breakup

Summary: "This book offers essential guidance on how to get over the emotional baggage of a breakup in order to be open to new love. It focuses on eight things you need to break up with in order to purge old emotional baggage and eliminate that unwanted attachment. Its specific steps will help clear your energy of the past so that the new can finally come in."—Provided by publisher.

ISBN: 979-8-9897773-8-9 (paperback)
1. Self Help 2. Relationships

Library of Congress Control Number: 2024906568

Manufactured in the United States of America

Contents

Dedication v

Prologue vii

Introduction 1

1 Breaking Up with Belongings 9

2 Breaking Up with Your Apartment or House 19

3 Breaking Up with Your Ex's Friends and Family 27

4 Breaking Up with Places You Frequented Together 31

5 Breaking Up with Old Pics, Social Media Posts,
 and Old Texts/Emails 37

6 Breaking Up with Old Energies of Intimacy 41

7 Breaking Up with Resentment and Regret (Do It for You) 45

8 Breaking Up with Old Dreams, Plans, and Wishes 51

Okay Universe! I'm Ready (for New Beginnings)
Whenever You Are! 57

8 *More* Little Bites of Wisdom as You Start a Deliciously
Amazing New Chapter of Your Life 59

Epilogue 61

Resources for Mental and Emotional Health 63

Index 65

Dedication

It didn't go as you expected.

You thought it would last forever.

You thought you had found the one.

You were left to mend your broken heart, by yourself,
though you're not the one who broke it.

I know how you feel.

I've been there.

But things are different now.

You know it's time to let go.

You know it's time to claim happiness, joy, and peace again.

It will take work. It will take change.

You will have to let go of people or things
that were once important to you.

It's part of the process.
The new can't come in until the old is fully released.

But you are ready. This is why you are here.
This is why we are here, for you.

The Universe is waiting on your signal
to activate blessings for your next life chapter.

Release the past fully, and make room for new beginnings.

You deserve the best. Do your part,
and watch life do its part too. It will amaze you.

Peace and love, always…

Mama Bear

Prologue

You swear you'll never rent a moving van again. Driving this vehicle on winding mountain roads is one of the most terrifying things you've ever done. It is also one of the hardest times of your life as memories, broken promises, shattered dreams, and a broken heart all lay scattered chaotically in the back of the van. Maybe for you it is a car. Or maybe it is just you, walking away, with nothing but the clothes on your back.

The whole ordeal takes about six hours. Then, just like that, it is all over. For you, yes, but not for the Universe, for it vows to balance things out for you in due time. It always did. It always does.

You're home. The door opens and you don't call their name. You don't hurry up to see what they are doing in the living room. For the first time in a long time, it's just you, alone, in your space. No "Hi babe, how was your day?" No "Dude, guess what happened at work today?" Nothing. Crickets. Just you, staring at a silent room which used to be full of laughter, talks, fights, and passionate makeup "sessions," if you know what I mean.

You put your house keys in their usual spot and go sit in yours: the recliner in the living room. You breathe and try to envision your new life without your ex. You try to plan your week without them. However, all you can focus on is your ex's scent still lingering on the throw laying on the arm of your recliner. And suddenly, the memories come flooding in.

You remember the last time your ex sat there. The last time they turned the TV on. Although your ex is out of the home physically, their energy seems to be in every room of your home. Their presence is still felt in every corner of your closet, in every seat of your car. You try to shake the memories off, and focus on planning your week, but you soon realize that you and your ex spent so much time together that you will think of them when you go to the gym later, when you order from the Thai place, when you take your morning walk by the park, and so on.

If you think: "It cannot be good for me to constantly be reminded of my ex," you're right. What we focus on becomes our reality, or better yet, stays in our reality. Having many reminders of past relationships keeps the energy of the old in the present and takes up mental space that should be filled by new beginnings, self-love, inner peace, and new dreams. Since there's only so much attention you can give to the different parts of your life, past relationship energy must leave to make room for new chapters. Does that mean you have to leave your old life behind, sell everything, unfriend everyone, and move to another country? Not at all. You may consider parting with certain people, places, and things, but there are ways to repackage what's left behind so that memories of the old don't haunt you forever and potentially block your new beginnings.

It's time to release old energies. It's time to free up your mental space. It's time to make room for the new beginnings life is so eager to send your way. It's time to set the stage to receive it all.

That is what this book is here to help you accomplish.

Introduction
The Hard Truth About "Uncoupling"

Two become one… and then become two again…

Don't worry! Plenty of fish in the sea! It's his loss! She'll never do better than you! You'll find someone better in no time! Forget about him!

How many times do you hear this after a breakup? Almost always. Often it comes from well-meaning friends and family who try to lift your spirits up, or people who truly believe the breakup was for the best. Other times, those sentiments are expressed by people who secretly wonder what's wrong with you for not making it work with your person, but want to be polite and say something nice.

However, no matter who says it to you and what their true feelings are, those words rarely provide any real sense of comfort and peace when your heart is reeling from one of the hardest things individuals can experience: breaking up with someone with whom you thought you'd spend the rest of your life.

TWO BECOME ONE… AND THEN BECOME TWO AGAIN

There are those who can easily "uncouple" in a friendly, peaceful manner, and who are able to find ways to let go of old relationships with ease. Although that is possible at any stage of a union, it may seem easier for romantic partnerships that are relatively new, for relationships which do not involve marriage or children, or for couples who do not jointly own assets, debt, and so forth.

That does not mean those types of relationships always end effortlessly and with no sadness. No. It just means that things get a little more complicated when lives have been merged in a multitude of ways, and more consequentially, over a multitude of years.

However, for a sizable majority of folks, maybe including you, me, and many others, a seamless and smooth "uncoupling" process is not always doable, as it is not always easy to create a clear path to full, clean separation.

Indeed, what others on the outside of your relationship may not grasp is that your ex was involved in every aspect of your current life. They were your automatic plus-one to events and social gatherings. Your family basically adopted them as another daughter, son, sister, uncle, and auntie. All your friends had their numbers as your "in-case-of-emergency" contact, and so did the people in your workplace. Every restaurant you liked knew their favorite meal and even had a special table for the two of you. Your day, week, month, and year consisted of coordinating your schedules to do as many things together as possible. "You and me against the world," you thought. A unit of two. One united front.

And then, the breakup happened, and alas, the united front was no more. One became two again and it was heartbreaking. Everything you thought was solid and stable in your life suddenly feels like it's falling apart right in front of your very eyes. You feel lost and unsure about how your life will look going forward, at least in the short term.

You may have been one of those people who saw the end coming as the relationship deteriorated over time, and therefore you may not have been completely shocked and surprised when it ended. However, you may have belonged to a category that many find themselves in, which is the group of folks who got blindsided, and found themselves having to pick up the pieces of broken promises, unachieved goals, and an unfulfilled love story.

Now what? How do you untangle two lives that were so intertwined? While many consider things done and over with the moment there is physical separation, it is not always that clear cut. Often, exes are not around in the flesh, but their presence can still be felt in more ways than one. Whether you remember them in their favorite recliner every time you come home, or they cross your mind every time you go to the restaurant where you met them for the first time, it sometimes seems impossible to totally erase your ex's energy from your life. It's like the ghost of lovers' past keeps hanging around you and you can't seem to shake them off. *Go away, already! Jeez…*

So, you ask again, how do you start rebuilding your life and moving on, while the energy of your ex is stitched into every piece of furniture, every restaurant you frequented, every kitchen plate, etc.?

One thing is for sure: You do not want to walk around life carrying the energy of old relationships because you know full well that the old must go in order for the new to arrive. Remember that expression, "Out with the old, and in with the new?" Well, it is a phrase that is commonly used for a reason. In order to attract new energy into your life, the old has to go. It is that simple. So, how do you do that?

Well, don't worry. I got you. You don't have to try to figure it out alone. I've created this book to answer this very question. However, before you dive into the steps you could take to fully release the energy of past relationships, take a moment to really grasp why it is so very important to do so.

The information you are about to receive is very crucial to creating the best conditions for you to attract new love into your life. *It is not a substitute for professional, medical, mental, or emotional advice,* but these suggestions may help you detach from past energies so you make way for new beginnings. So, please take your time and read everything that follows with your full attention.

YOUR EX IS NOT PHYSICALLY WITH YOU. BUT IS THEIR ENERGY STILL AROUND?

Okay. It's over. You've tried your best, and maybe your partner tried their best too. However, it did not work out and you know for sure that your relationship now is done for good. You are officially no longer together. You don't go out together, you are no longer each other's emergency contacts, you don't even see each other, or talk to each other. You both go about your lives and your ex is out of your system. It's all done, right?

Well, not necessarily. The Energy of your old relationship may still be lingering around and impacting your life even if you are not aware of it.

The importance of detaching energetically

In recent years, there has been a renewed focus on the energy of people, places, and things, and on how energy plays into the life of every individual. We remember the quote from world-renowned physicist and scientist Albert Einstein: "Everything is energy and that's all there is to it… This is not philosophy. This is physics." Many interpret this statement as explaining that everything in life and every experience one goes through carries with it an energetic vibration. If that is so, even if an ex is out of one's immediate environment, there may still be certain things in that environment that carry their vibration and keep it active in there. In other words, exes may not be around, but their energy may still linger in items left behind, the places you visit, or any of your activities.

This famous quote from global personal development expert Tony Robbins ties it all together: "Where focus goes, energy flows." That is powerful and true. If being around certain things or situations constantly shifts your attention to the past relationship, your focus will continue to be on it and not on what you want to manifest for the next phase of your life. The old energies may even conflict with your efforts to bring new vibes into your world.

If you don't think energy can linger in the absence of the object it is originally attributed to, consider this. Some say that they can just drive by a beach where they made lots of great memories years ago, and still feel happy in the present moment without stepping foot on the sand. They say that this happens because some memories still carry the energetic imprint/feeling of the old experience. In other words, just the thought of the beach alone can bring back the pleasant feelings that it generated in the people years ago, without them having to experience that location in person again. So amazing, and perhaps so scary too.

Nowadays, there are talks, classes, and discussions about energy, energy clearing, and energy healing. In fact, in March 2017 PBS reported that "top medical research centers such as Duke, John Hopkins, and Yale offer "energy healing" to help treat a variety of illnesses.[1] We hear about the energetic healing properties of crystals and minerals, about the energetic healing properties of nature, metals, animals, and other things. There are many books, seminars, and workshops on the importance of surrounding oneself with people with positive energy and staying away from those with so-called negative, or low-vibrating, energy. Those topics have been researched, spoken about, and written about for decades, centuries, and beyond, from every corner of the world.

Since energy is attached to everything in life, when individuals are in a committed union and have been for a while, there is no doubt that there will be an interaction of energy between them. Bestselling American author and lecturer Bruce Lipton stated in a YouTube video that "everything is an energy field with no borders to it…"[2] He followed up with the idea that one's energy can affect or even cancel another's energy.

So, in relationships, where each partner will bring their own "energetic signature" to the union, energy will undoubtedly flow back and forth from one party to the next. There are even cases in which couples are so in sync that it feels like they can feel each other's emotions when they are apart and may even hear each other's thoughts without anyone uttering a single word. Now, that's the real manifestation of the phrase, "two become one," isn't it?

If you are in a union, the energy that flows between you and your partner in a relationship can permeate every aspect of your lives together. It can be felt or found in the places that you stay together, in your heart, in your mind, in your body, in your soul, and even in objects you bought together or objects that were special to the relationship. That energy can be found in the friend groups that you both shared, in the vacation

---

[1] https://www.pbs.org/newshour/health/top-u-s-hospitals-promote-unproven-medicine-side-mysticism
[2] https://www.youtube.com/watch?v=Zy-vkYQz12Q

locations that you visited together, and even in the grocery store where you both shopped on Sunday mornings. Some even say that old energy shared during intimacy can stay in the cells of your body for a long time, and if not released properly can interfere in your intimacy with the next person you are with. I will discuss that a little later in the book.

So, does all of this mean that you will always carry the energy of old relationships with you and that you will be energetically attached to your ex forever? No. Don't worry. Although some of that energy will remain in your memories, it will not have the same impact on you as when you were in that relationship… *but if, and only if, you take the right steps to properly release it!*

Those steps are not always easy, but meaningful change requires serious action. Without getting rid of old energies, it becomes very difficult to create space for new ones to come in, as I mentioned earlier. We hear many stories of people who said they broke up with their partners and did everything to find new love, but that new love was just not showing up. While there can be many reasons for that (ranging from "not putting yourself out there," to not healing some inner wounds that may be blocking love from entering your being), one of the common themes that surfaces in relationship discussions is that people are still somewhat energetically attached to their exes, even after full physical separation.

That is what we call *energetic attachment*, and that is what this book aims to help you finally get rid of, once and for all. A "clean break" is a sign of strength, not weakness.

You don't need to prove to anyone (including yourself) that you are strong.

Before diving into the "eight things" you must break up with after your breakup, I must stress a very important point when it comes to moving forward in life after a separation.

YOU DON'T HAVE TO PROVE TO ANYONE THAT YOU ARE STRONG (according to their definition of strength).

I want to stress this because often people do not seek guidance or help to rebuild their lives after hardship because they feel the need to appear strong.

Please seek professional help if you feel you need assistance with managing your emotions after a breakup or other types of hardships or emotional upheaval. The end of this book includes mental health and emotional health resources that you can use if you feel they could benefit you in any way. You do not have to tell everyone you know that you are struggling with your recent breakup, or that you are going to therapy to deal with your separation or divorce. However, *please do not be ashamed to tell your truth*. Own your truth, and please don't fear telling people about it if you so choose. You never know who you may inspire to seek help for themselves after hearing you are vulnerable. It is a sign of strength to gather the resources you need to live your best life—physically, emotionally, and mentally.

Indeed, taking steps to clear your mental and emotional energy of any past baggage, romantic or not, is an act of self-love, good mental health, and self-care. It is everyone's duty and responsibility to protect their energetic space as much as possible to ensure that the people, places, and things that one allows in one's own life bring joy, happiness, and peace.

Nobody wants constant reminders of failure, loss, sadness, and disappointment, whether those reminders are obvious or subtle. In any case, they keep people in low vibrational states that are not conducive to inner joy, inner peace, gratitude, or happiness. Low vibrational feelings can also often have physiological ramifications, such as stress, which can affect physical health in a variety of negative ways.

ON TO THE EIGHT THINGS

Once you understand the very important issue of energy and how it relates to making a clean break from the past, it is time to proceed into the eight things you should break up with after your breakup. Please keep an open mind and understand these steps are a guide for you, but they are no substitute for the answers lying in your own inner wisdom, or for professional advice.

My goal is to present you with perspectives that are aimed at activating your own inner wisdom and inner guidance so that you can create the framework that best fits your unique set of circumstances, as you create a path to the next chapter of your life after your breakup.

It is your decision as to how to navigate your next steps, and it is my mission to share crucial and transformative information with you so that your future can be as bright, as beautiful, and as fulfilling as it can be.

The steps in this book are for you, to guide you through your journey back to love, self-love, self-empowerment, and universal/divine love. May you find and enjoy it all for the rest of your life!

Why are you still wearing your ex's t-shirt anyway?

1 · **Breaking Up with Belongings**

It's over. No getting back together. Finished. Done. Okay. After being in your feelings for a bit—crying, getting angry, getting sad, feeling lost—you gather yourself and focus on one of the first things you need to do to untangle a partnership that was part of your identity: separating belongings.

You gather a few friends or close family to help you get your stuff out of your ex's place, or the place you shared together, or your ex got their stuff out of your place or your mutual place. Sounds complicated because it can be complicated… and also very traumatic, unfortunately.

Indeed, one of the hardest parts of a breakup is the moving/handling/disposing of belongings tied to the relationship. Most couples who had reached the point of being labeled as being in a committed, long-term relationship usually either live together or spend time regularly at each other's places, unless it is a long-distance thing. This means that each party will have to now decide what to do with items that represent aspects of the relationship. So, what do you do then?

Well, the tough love and hard truth is that *ideally* the best thing would be to GET RID OF IT ALL!

Now, it is obvious that this cannot be achieved in most situations. The most serious scenarios involve a family home in which the couple's children may live, a pet the kids love with all their hearts, a minivan that the custodial parent needs to use to bring the kids back and forth to school, vacation homes, etc. Although many of those items end up remaining in the family for practical reasons, there are still ways to reduce their energetic ties to the past relationship. That is the point, remember? *Releasing the energy attached to the old relationship.* If you happen to be in the category of people who have items that are more difficult and less practical to separate from, do not worry. There is hope. We will cover that in a little bit.

Please note that I do not address the handling of custody of children in this book. The topic of children is a personal, sensitive, delicate, and important area that needs to be handled with love, compromise, and peace, with the children's best interest as the priority for each parent involved.

For couples who do not have mutually owned possessions such as the ones described prior, there are still many belongings that stem from past partnerships such as clothes and gifts. Also, partners may own things that they used for certain special occasions with their partners, such as dresses, suits, shoes, jewelry, and other personal items.

Whether the belongings in question are big-ticket items that are more difficult or less practical to give away or replace, or whether they are possessions that are easier to dispose of, it remains a fact that all relationship-related belongings carry energy from the old union. One look at the dress you got engaged in can bring sadness or anger to your heart. That's energy and not always happy energy. Every time you see that dress in your closet, although you may not be conscious of it, it may affect your emotions or your vibe, generally not in a positive way. In general, old clothing items that were of particular significance to an old relationship carry with them memories that are still, energetically speaking, trapped in your closet, and therefore trapped in your mind, trapped in your life, and possibly trapped in your heart.

Another example can be the gym clothes your ex-partner gave you for your birthday. It's not only that you love the outfits and that they fit well. Perhaps they also get you noticed by many good looking gym members. And that is a good thing, right (especially now that you are single)? So, why would you change that? Well, all is great and dandy when you wear them, except for the fact that when you put them on, they sometimes bring a tear to your eye when you remember the way you felt when you opened your birthday present that day. Or they may bring anger at the thought of the betrayal that your ex inflicted upon you. Either way, it's *no bueno*.

Other than clothes, there are kitchen items, bed sheets, towels, jewelry, car decorations, home decorations, the paintings you bought together, and any number of other shared items, all carrying the energy of the past union. So, do you have to get rid of them all to release the associated energy from your life?

The hard truth is that the answer is: Yes!

Break up with them all if you can. Well, let's say break up with them "as much as possible," okay? Indeed, one should at least try to get rid of as many things as doable that relate to the old union.

In March 2023 psychologist James Travers was cited on Forbes.com as recommending that after a breakup you should: "Leave all reminders of your ex in the dust." Indeed, he elaborated by adding that exes should find the courage to "purge" their space of each other's stuff and to "box up any physical reminders."[3]

Before you start hyperventilating when thinking about having to get rid of the Louis Vuitton Bag your ex bought you for your birthday, or the leather jacket they got you for the holidays, take a deep breath and don't panic. Consider the practical way of determining what you would be wise to let go of, and what can stay, under certain circumstances.

To begin, remember the two categories of belongings I mentioned above. The items that are easier to replace and the ones that may not be as easy to part with for various reasons. Also remember that *everything carries an energetic footprint*, and that the point of our discussion here is to ensure *you do not block new energy from entering your life* by keeping too much of the old energy around you and your space. So first, consider things you may want to get rid of and can part with relatively easily.

---

[3] https://www.forbes.com/sites/traversmark/2023/03/03/a-psychologist-reveals-4-ways-to-heal-and-move-on-after-a-breakup/?sh=7b813f9c1a47

YOUR BELONGINGS BREAKUP LIST

No matter how cute the wine glass set is, if you bought it with your ex, chances are that looking at it will bring back memories you may not want to think about. Or it may bring fuzzy feelings that bring you back to good times you enjoyed with your ex. Either way, being around the cute wine glasses can bring the energy of your ex back into your mental space. Is that what you want? If not, why do you still have them?

Here are some things to consider when it comes to relationship-related belongings, and why you may still be holding on to them:

You do not want the expense of replacing the items.

That is understandable, especially today, when the world recently went through a pandemic that affected the economic resources of many. While many can sympathize with anyone's desire to not spend money on things that do not need to be replaced, ask yourself: What is the price you would put on achieving emotional healing from your breakup and feeling inner peace? What is the price of possibly blocking new love by having too many items triggering memories of a past that you desperately want to leave behind? Is holding on to old belongings worth it? What is the choice or course of action that is more closely related to your self-love? Holding on to the old or letting them go? Something to think about...

You want to seem strong and show that you can handle the memories of the past. I touched on this a bit a few pages ago. Indeed, a common expectation after breakups is that former partners show strength when it comes to being around their exes or being around things that may bring their memories to the forefront. We often hear of people purposely wearing clothes that their exes loved in hope of making them jealous if they see them wearing the outfits. Furthermore, some feel it is a sign of weakness to feel emotional when being around items that may remind them of their exes, so they keep them around just to prove their mental and emotional fortitude to others. Meanwhile, on the inside, they may be breaking little by little because they are trying to feel feelings of detachment that are not ready to come up yet.

You want to show off the items your ex bought you to get a rise out of your ex's new partner.
Now, no one is calling anyone out, but if that's you, then you *know* it's you. And you know that this type of behavior and mindset cannot be good for your mental and emotional health in the long term. While it may bring some temporary low-quality, short-lived satisfaction, caring that much about the reaction of your ex's new person is a clear sign that you have not moved on and that you are holding on to old energy with a vengeance. It is an indication of work that needs to be done on the self-love and self-respect aspects of your heart and mind.

BREAKING UP WITH THE HARDER THINGS

As I noted earlier, there are some things that are harder and less practical to part with. So, what can you do to decrease or release the energetic bonds of belongings related to the old relationship? Here are a few suggestions:

Make a list of the belongings you can part with and those you can't.
This is hard, but you must courageously make a list of things you can part with, as well as those you can't—at least not in the present moment. This is something you must be honest with yourself about. It is easy to say, "I really need those shoes they bought me," or "I cannot replace the expensive work shirts they got me." There is always going to be a reason for keeping items around, and it is up to you to be strong and let go of what can be replaced with no big investment or action. If the belongings involve big-ticket items such as a home or a car, refer to the advice in the next section. No worries! For now, just focus on the things that are more easily replaceable.

One factor that can make your decisions easier is thinking about those who are in need of the items you can part with. Whether you decide to sell some items or donate others, the same applies to how the recipient of your items may feel, and it is most likely going to be a happy feeling. That brings warmth to the heart of anyone who is on the giving end of the item. As the saying goes, "It's in giving that we receive."

So go ahead and make a donate/sell list and commit to it. Remember that many times holding on to things is an emotional decision rather than a needs-based decision. Often, once we spend a few days without an item, we learn to live without it and eventually forget about it all altogether. Make someone happy by donating what you can or make some money by getting rid of belongings from past relationships. Either way, you win! Winning!

If you really cannot part with something, there are two questions to ask yourself:

Question #1: "Am I holding on to the item because it reminds me of the love my ex and I shared?"

If the answer is yes, BREAK UP WITH IT! Your ex now has that status for a reason, and if you are still reminiscing about the love that you shared, or if you are still sad over the breakup, then you cannot hold on to things that remind you of that love. *That love is gone.* Holding on to such things is not good for your mental and emotional health. It also works against you energetically speaking if you are trying to attract new love. The energies of love, regret, and sadness are very strong and can affect you in deeper ways than you can imagine.

If you find yourself holding onto items from a past relationship as a means to remember that relationship, because you have hope of rekindling something you know is done (and done), then you need to find the courage to get rid of those. It may be hard at first, but holding on to items out of those feelings cannot be good for anyone. And if you say, "Well, what if my ex comes back and gets upset that I got rid of the belongings that were meaningful to the relationship?" Well, if by chance you and your ex get back together, you can acquire new items together that will not have the energy of your old, failed relationship attached to them. Doesn't that sound like something that would be a good thing? It does because it is. GET RID OF IT!

Question #2: "If I am sure I am *not* holding on to some belongings due to emotions that inhibit my self-love or ability to move on, then how do I keep them while releasing their energies of the past?"

Maybe you remember that Louis Vuitton bag your ex gave you last Christmas. And the expensive watch they gave you for your birthday. We know about the car they bought for you last year, and the golf clubs they gave you to celebrate your retirement. Again, don't panic! No one is asking you to be unrealistic with your money by getting new things unnecessarily (if you are not holding on to them out of sentimental value). So, what can you do about them, energetically speaking? Well, please allow me to welcome you to consider the following options:

Thoroughly, mindfully, and intentionally cleanse the items you are keeping!

Here are some ways you can achieve this step. If you are into saging (the practice of burning dried sage leaves to cleanse the air of negative energy), then sage the old energy out of the old belongings you cannot part with at this time! And feel free to shout as you are doing so: "Get out, you are no longer welcomed here, you have no power here, go away. I release any relationship energy attached to those items that are tied to the past. I release old energies to the wind and the sea and the stars." You get the idea. But please remember safety first when saging: Make sure you get training on how to safely sage your space, make sure it is allowed in your house or apartment, and please open windows to let the smoke out. Also make sure you or other household members or neighbors have no medical issues with burning sage.

If you are not into saging, or cannot do it for one reason or another, you can either hire a cleaning crew, or take time to cleanse the remaining belongings yourself if you are able to. Some people recommend using natural cleaning items in your cleaning water such as lavender, lemon, lime, orange, dried flowers, cinnamon, vanilla, etc., if you are not allergic. Before you clean, set an intention to release old energy, beliefs, and feelings, which no longer serve you and make room for good vibes to surround your items. You can even say the words we mentioned above out loud as you are cleaning the stuff. Remember to focus on the new, so do not think "good riddance, old energies," but rather focus on new happy vibes. Do everything joyfully, as much as possible.

Bring in some fresh air...literally.
If you choose not to sage or clean, though cleaning is highly recommended, just open your windows when the weather permits, and say the things we mentioned out loud, while visualizing in your mind the new vibes pouring out of your old belongings.

Change the story of the belongings you choose to keep.
In other words, choose to assign a different meaning to those items than the one they had in the past. This is a powerful tool. For example, if you wore a beautiful green dress to a surprise birthday party that your ex threw for you for your thirtieth birthday, and you feel that the dress does not bring you sadness or regret (and you really like it because you bought it years ago, before the ex and their fakery, and it fits so nicely, and makes you look hot), wear it for an occasion that brings you joy and that marks a great day in your life.

From that moment, every time you look at the dress and wear it, tell yourself, "wow, this is the dress I accepted this award in," or "this is the dress I wore when I got my promotion." Words have power. When you change the way you speak of an item, you basically can change its karma or energy by renaming it and reframing what it means in your life. This is high-level subconscious mindset rewiring, Jedi mastery stuff, guys, and it works. We can change our lives by the way we speak of things and the perspective we have on things. Remember what Dr. Wayne Dyer said: "If we change the way we look at things, the things we look at will change."

Now, this mindset-shifting business is not an easy feat and requires a lot of emotional mastery and healing, but it is doable. Often, you are only able to do this paradigm reframing after the grieving period of losing a relationship, and after getting to a mental and emotional space where you understand that what is meant to stay in your life *will* stay; and what does not stay after some effort was only there for a short time. Healing takes time and that's OKAY. You don't become a Jedi or Master right away; it takes training.

Because this process takes some time, you may find yourself unable to look at some belongings in this new way. No worries. In that case, leave them aside for a while, preferably somewhere you cannot see them every day, and give yourself time to heal. If after a certain time you still cannot come to the point where you can happily be around the items in question, then GET RID OF THEM. There is nothing worth you feeling sad or regretful. If something cannot bring you joy after a while, then let it go, even if it hurts like hell to part with it. I've been there and I have felt my heart splitting while donating certain items that were so dear to me. However, the thought of them kept bringing me back to negative feelings, so I chose my peace at the end of the day.

Side note: I can say honestly that I've never regretted giving "old relationship belongings" away. Ever. I even forgot some of the things I parted with. Many things, actually. Trust me, you will too.

So, what do you think? Are there old belongings from past relationships that you are holding on to? Do you feel the energy of the past relationship when you are around those items? Get close to them and close your eyes for a bit. Listen to how your body feels and what thoughts come through your mind. Then open your eyes and look at the items. Do you still want them in your energetic field? Only you can answer that question and only you will know what to do.

So what's the moral of the story here? Well, it is that whatever you decide, go for the option that gives you inner peace. Your heart will thank you.

Is your space really your space, or yours and your ex's space?

2 · **Breaking Up with Your Apartment or House**

Once upon a time, there lived a beautiful maiden who had her own place, all cute, magical, and put together. On the other side of town lived a handsome young lad who had his bachelor pad, all slick, with dark furniture, a room for his beloved German Shepherd, Buddy, and another room just for his gym equipment. Then one day, the maiden and the lad crossed paths, their eyes met, and it was love at first sight. Within hours they discovered that they could not be apart from each other for too long. It felt like air wooshed out of the room when one of them left the other.

So, they decided to get rid of their respective abodes and get a place together. They found the perfect apartment or house in which they could see themselves living happily ever after. Before long they no longer spoke of his place, or their place. It was "our space." Awww…the things we do for love…

Until the day they broke up. He moved out, and she was left in a house which smelled of him, smelled of his dog that they had loved like their own, and was full of walls that had been painted by him. Or perhaps the story was that they walked out and broke up with *him*, leaving them heartbroken, in an apartment that still featured the light fixtures they picked out, the wine glasses they collected from endless tasting events, and a master bedroom whose main wall still had their initials on it, right in the center of a heart that they painted together. Ugh, so silly. (Well, it felt cute back then!)

Shoot…Now what?

How do you get rid of past relationship energy attached to every wall, every fixture, every tile? Well, you have two main options. Let's explore them both.

GET OUT OF DODGE!

Yes, get out! Move! Yes! Break up with the old space. Well, the question is, are you able to move and can you find a place that's convenient for you and makes you happy? Again, breakups usually come with sadness and inconvenience and actions one wishes one would not have to take. So, having to go through a few unstable weeks or months to reset your life and relocate may suck for a little while, but it should not be a reason to stay in a place that brings up too many memories of the past, even if they are pleasant memories. Remember, any energetic attachment, whether it brings up happy thoughts or unhappy thoughts, is still ATTACH-MENT! The point of it all is to release that attachment and purge your energy of all that pulls your own energy backwards. So, put your big girl or big boy pants on and do what needs to be done. GET OUT!

The space we reside in and go to every day has a huge impact on our mental health. It should be a sacred place where we are surrounded by items which invoke feelings of peace, joy, and happiness in our hearts and minds. A 2018 online *Psychology Today* article written by Chloe Carmichael, Ph.D., states that, "Decorating to make your home a psychological comfort zone is not a luxury; it is core to your well-being."[4] Indeed, since our surroundings directly affect our emotions, by extension they can also affect our physical health. What we feel in our emotional body on the inside often, if not always, gets reflected in what we feel in our physical body on the outside. That is why people say things such as, "This makes me sick to my stomach," when something displeases them in any significant way.

When you open the door to your place, you should ideally feel peace and joy, but at the very least, peace. The same goes for where you lay

---

[4] https://www.psychologytoday.com/us/blog/the-high-functioning-hotspot/202008/the-ultimate-guide-breakups

your head at night and where you sit down to have your breakfast or dinner, and even your bathroom. If your place constantly takes you back to moments of a relationship you are trying to forget or put behind you, you may be energetically blocking yourself from welcoming new love or new energy into your life. It also may fill you with sadness, anger or resentment, which act as an energetic repellent for new loving energies to make their way to you.

Again, there always will be reasons to justify not going through the trouble of moving and finding a new home or apartment. However, you must be careful not to confuse legitimate reasons with excuses.

At the end of the day, is the discomfort you may feel by having to move worse than the everyday angst of remembering a time in your life you'd rather forget?

Sometimes we just have to go for the lesser of two evils (or what we feel is evil). Usually, however, that is not the case. The way we see things is just a projection of either love or fear that we already carry inside towards the two so-called "evil" options. But you get the point, right? It may feel uncomfortable and even somewhat uncertain to pack up and restart your life in a different place, but remember that every ending is a new beginning. Don't you deserve to give yourself a new beginning?

IMAGINE WHAT WILL MAKE YOU HAPPY

Do this exercise:

Imagine yourself in a place that you can call yours. What color would you paint the walls? What neighborhood would you be living in? It can be the same as the one you resided in before, but maybe it can be on another street. What about the other areas in town you like? Or the city you heard speaks more to your spirit? What would be the first thing you'd want to see when you walk in the door? (Remember, it needs to be something that makes your heart smile.) What would it be? What are some of the décor items you would like to have in your living room?

Maybe you had considered getting a tiny house in Colorado or a flat in England? What if this is the universe giving you the opportunity to live abroad for a year, like you've always dreamed of? Can't you see the opportunities that this (breakup) moment in your life is presenting to you? Why would you want to be in a place where you didn't give yourself a chance to experience them? Think about that...

Now, I know you may really wish you could move and leave everything behind. However, you may have very good reasons (not excuses) for wishing to stay in the space where you resided with your ex. Perhaps it is close to your job and makes life very convenient for you. Or maybe the house is in your name, and it is a good investment that you do not want to forfeit, especially after you had to pay your ex off via financial settlement for their interest in the home. It may be that you guys have kids, want to give them some type of stability after the breakup, and wish to allow them and yourself to stay in the house they know or grew up in.

Certainly, there could be hundreds of legitimate reasons, financial or otherwise, for you to want to stay in a place you shared with your ex.

IF YOU STAY: PURGING THE OLD ENERGY

If you can't move and change your place of residence after sharing it with an ex, you can bring in new energy, thus forcing the old energy to get out of your space.

So how do you get rid of as much old relationship energy as possible when you remain in a place you shared together? One beneficial and impactful step you can take is changing the appearance of your place by giving it a facelift. This can be done with small changes or big changes depending on your budget, and available time and resources.

Thoroughly, mindfully, and intentionally cleanse your space!

Yup, I said it again. Do it for your belongings AND for your space. "If you are into saging, and "only" IF you have learned from professionals how to do it properly and safely, then sage the old energy out of the old space, even rooms your ex did not spend time in.

Feel free to shout the same things you said when it came to saging your belongings as you are doing so: "Get out past energy. I release you fully and completely. You are not welcomed here. You have no power here. Go away. I release any energy of the past that may be attached to the walls, the grounds, the items in the home, the doors, the air, the plants, and grass and concrete around the home and the neighborhood. I release all old energies (that do not serve the greater good for my life) to the wind and the sea and the stars, and the Sun and the Moon, etc."

You get the idea, right? Please remember again that safety is the number-one priority when saging. Make sure it is legally allowed in your house or apartment, and please open windows to let the smoke out. Also make sure you or other household members or neighbors have no medical issues or other issues with burning sage.

Again, if you choose not to sage, just open your windows, and say the things I mentioned out loud, while visualizing in your mind that the old energy is coming out of your space through the windows and/or doors. Then close the windows and doors and say, "buh-bye."

IMPORTANT—READ CAREFULLY:

I briefly mentioned this earlier but want to reiterate it because it is crucial information. When you intentionally engage in vocally or mentally releasing energy, you must do so from a place of inner peace and self-love. If you are out there screaming to the energy to get out with anger and frustration and ill intent towards your ex , then that is the energy that you will embody, thus the energy that you will attract. Do any release with the focus on loving yourself, not with the focus on blaming anyone, bashing anyone, or punishing anyone. If you are still in that frame of mind as you are trying to release old energy from your life, you may need to do some healing work, some inner work of forgiveness and surrender. I'll tell you about that later in the book, no worries.

TRANSFORM THE LOOK AND DESIGN OF YOUR PLACE

If you opt for giving your place the proverbial facelift, here are some things you can do.

Move furniture around.

A space can be transformed just by moving some things around and possibly replacing some furniture. If your ex had a favorite recliner where they sat all the time watching football, or a lounge chair where they sat every evening to read their e-books, it may be best to get rid of it, if you can. If you guys had a chair where you, hmmm…you know, did certain "spicy" things, GET RID OF IT! You would not want a potential future partner to sit on that, would you now? The same way you wouldn't want to sit on a similar chair at the home of a potential future partner for you, right?

For the other furniture such as your bedroom set, try your best to move things around and change the look of the room. I personally recommend changing at least the mattress where you both laid together, if you used it a lot, or maybe flipping it over after giving it a good scrub or steam. One thing that should be common sense would be at least to get yourself new bed sheets. Even if you wash your old ones really well, no respectable new love interest wants to lay down on bed sheets on which you and your old partner did the deed. If your new potential mate does not care, ask yourself what may be hiding in the sheets of their bed when you go to their place. Just saying.

For your living room and dining room sets, it may be more difficult to move that furniture around, so just do your best.

Redecorate your space.

It is amazing how changing a few decorative pillows, some curtains, certain area rugs, some kitchen décor items, your sofa covers, one or two throws you use in your den, your bathroom mats, your wall décor items, etc., can make a place feel like new. With the infinite amount of home décor items available in stores and online, and at relatively affordable prices, it is not that difficult at all to change the look of your abode. You can experiment with color schemes, with patterns, with different types of styles from bohemian (one of my favorites), to modern, to rustic, to farmhouse, and so on.

A quick trip to the fabric store, craft store, or home décor retailer can help you give your space a makeover that will not only remove the feel of the past, but also give you joy, as you bring in new elements that make your heart happy and fill you with peace. There is an almost childlike joy that can fill you up when you get to decorate your space and make it reflect the light you carry inside you. Just the process of decoration alone brings you joy, and that feeling only intensifies every time you open your front door and step into your sacred space. By the time you are done, you may not even remember what it looked like before, as you will be so excited to talk about the changes you made and how they make you feel.

Doing this changes your focus from the past to the present—and can bring you happiness. By feeling happiness, you automatically transform the energy of your space and your inner space, and that attracts happiness right back to you. Try it!

Repaint your space.

One additional thing you can do to remove old energy is to paint the interior walls to change the entire look of your home. Sometimes, due to budget constraints and maybe the layout of your space, or the rules of your building/complex, you may not be able to repaint your entire house or apartment. Nevertheless, consider creating an accent wall, for example, by painting only one wall instead of an entire room. That can make a big difference. Also, think about painting your kitchen cabinets, if doable or if allowed, if you don't own your space. You can also try repainting your backyard fence, or smaller rooms, such as your office or inside your garage.

DON'T FORGET YOUR CAR!

Yes, one of the places old energies can still remain is in your car, assuming you and your ex used to use it a lot to get around. Feel free to sage the car as well, if you could do it safely, or vocally release the old energies from it the way we discussed earlier. Some who are religious sometimes bring the car to their priests or pastors to have it blessed. That can also apply to your space, should you choose to bring someone or a group of fellow church members to say a special healing prayer there and bless the new phase of the place. Do whatever rocks your boat. For your car, you can also change the mats and the seat covers, give it a good vacuuming, or take it to be detailed.

If your ex frequently came to your office, feel free to change things around as I discussed above for your space, including rearranging furniture, replacing some décor and adding inspirational items that speak of your ideal life or ideal state of mind. *Remember, small changes can make a big difference.*

So, the moral of the story here? Move if you can, and if you cannot, change the look and feel of your surroundings. The happier you feel in your space and the more it makes you think of the present and future, and not the past, the better it is for you, and the quicker you can release any old energy attached to it (and by association, attached to you).

Were they your friends, your ex's friends?
Or just friends of the couple?

3 · Breaking Up with Your Ex's Friends and Family

Remember the last Thanksgiving? Or Friendsgiving, as you guys called it? When you, your ex, and all of your friends celebrated that special holiday at your place? You laughed and talked about the vacations you all took together, the crazy evenings where you all watched the football games at one another's houses, the drunken nights that you all are still trying to piece together years later, and so on. Remember Jeremy and his dog Rex, and Kyle and his wife Lauren, and Jamal and his sister Sandra, and Raj and his brother Sanjay? Do you remember all your old friends, or should I say, all your ex's friends who became your friends by…association?

Well, what happens now? You are no longer with your ex, but you still have all of his friends on your phone and still have some of their upcoming events on your calendar. So, what do you do?

Can you relate to this conundrum? Although some people don't find it difficult to navigate through the web of connections that can become rather uncertain after a breakup (don't really know who these lucky people are, lol), most individuals experience a certain amount of doubt and confusion when it comes to maintaining friendships with friends of their ex. Let's try to untangle this web by first identifying some of the types of friends we are talking about.

FRIENDS BY ASSOCIATION

First, you have your friends and family members who became your ex's friends because of your ex's association with you. Some of those friends are the "ride-or-die" type friends, who tolerated your partner only because you guys were an item. The same applies to your ex's ride-or-die friends, who really don't have a deep connection with you and were just "around" when you and your ex were together. There is usually no issue with trying to figure out how to manage those connections post breakup, as those types of connections follow their respective loyalty and exit your life or your ex's life as quickly as either of you say, "it's over," to which their answer is, "next." Wow! Savage. But everyone needs one (or more) ride-or-die friends, right?

CLOSER FRIENDS

Then you have the friends or family members who actually spent time with you one-to-one, even when your ex was not around. You felt like you could possibly remain friends, no matter where your relationship went or how it ended up. So, how do you manage those relationships? Well, I say, "BREAK UP WITH THEM!" (Ok…only under certain conditions.)

Let's explore that. Do you remember the main healing message of this book? It is to do whatever it takes to remove as much energy from the past as possible, so that you can make room for new beginnings and new energies to enter and enrich your life. Please keep that in mind.

That said, how you manage your relationships with your ex's friends and family with whom you have become close will depend on how much the interaction with them brings you back to feelings connected to your past relationship with your ex.

Here are some things to consider that can assist you in making your decision on how to proceed:

These friends have the right to decide for themselves.

What I mean by that is that it is a good idea to wait and see who reaches out to you after a breakup. If you reach out first, you may put the friend or family in an uncomfortable spot where they may feel obligated to talk to you though they may not be *ready* for that, or not yet feel comfortable enough to do so. Please keep in mind that no one knows the full details of your relationship with your ex, aside from you both, and friends and family may not know who was right or wrong, or who to support or not. Of course, we can assume that people will support their own sides, but that is not always the case.

However, it is good to be compassionate and not put people in a situation where they may feel the need to say something to you while they are not sure of what happened with your relationship. It is best to wait and see, allowing people to not contact you right away, or even ever. We all have free will and do what we feel is best for our mental health, emotional health, and social needs. Therefore, we must also respect others' rights to do the same and not resent them for exiting our life if that is what they choose to do. Remember, some are in our lives for a season and some for the long haul. Don't force anyone to stay when it is their time to go. Release them with peace.

The friends/family have the right to not want to take a side.

Again, people have free will and we all need to respect that, as we want others to respect our right to do what we want to do. The individuals who are not ride-or-die may actually like both you and your ex and feel they do not want to take a side. Although you may not ask them to do so and you are even very understanding about their allegiance to your ex, people may feel like they are "expected" to take a side and thus they try to avoid any conversation with the ex that was not from their side. Although human nature likes to feel supported and loved, it is important to allow people to not want to sit in your corner, should they choose not to.

So, what do you do then?

Now, we get to the main consideration of this section. The main question and the only one which really matters in the grand scheme of things, is: "How is being close to your ex's friends/family making you feel?"

When you find yourself around the individuals referred to above, do you feel that the conversation always goes back to your ex? Even if the sentiment being expressed is one of support for you, is the energy of the interaction one that makes you look backward, or forward? Does it focus on your joy, your healing, your future, your happiness, or does it highlight the loss, the regret, the missed opportunity of the relationship that just fizzled out?

This is not about the people being bad or having bad energy. That is not what I am alluding to here at all. It is about whether the interactions help or hurt your mental health, emotional health, and your efforts to move forward with your life and release past energy. Sometimes we remove certain people from our lives or remove ourselves from certain situations, not because they carry ill intent towards us, or are determined to damage us intentionally in any way, but because they are not compatible with our life's direction and with the actions we are taking to be our best selves, to practice self-care, and to let go of energies that are not helping us move forward. As spiritual leader, author, and personal development expert Deepak Chopra says: "In the process of letting go, you'll lose many things from the past, but you will find yourself."

As I noted earlier in this book, in life our obligation is to care for our hearts, minds, bodies, and spirits. If something or someone does not support that obligation, it is our duty to move away from that energy, but to do so with peace and without resentment or anger or ill intent.

Ask yourself: Is it more important for you to be surrounded by a big group of people, or is it quality over quantity? Is it more important for you to feel peace and joy and excitement and hope for the future, or for your ex's friends to still like you? If the answer is that your inner peace matters more, then don't be afraid to break up with any family/friend/connection that stands in the way of you moving forward.

So, what is the moral of this story? It is that you do not owe anyone an apology for protecting your emotional health. If you want to send someone a note stating you are taking some me-time and not interacting with many people at the moment, feel free to do so. However, you do not *owe* anyone an explanation for what you feel you must do to be OK on the inside. Those who truly care for you will give you the space to heal and will be there when you are ready to talk again, or they will respect your wishes if you decide to turn the page on some old connections, for good.

Does the restaurant bring back memories of your ex?

4 · Breaking Up with Places You Frequented Together

(Except the calamari place, lol).

Do you remember where you both used to sit when you came to have dinner in this restaurant? And what you each used to order? Even when you just came for takeout, or when you took your mom and dad there, do you recall how the first thing everyone asked you was how your partner was doing? What about the pet shop where you and your ex used to go to get food for your beloved goldfish? Or your cute (but batshit crazy) cat? It seemed like they liked your ex more than you. Remember the last time you went there, and they all gushed over them? Or when the cashier couldn't stop asking you about how you met and how long you've been together?

Well, it's been weeks since you've broken up and you've been to those places a couple of times and could not avoid the people who never saw you alone. They always saw you and your ex coming together and leaving together. For the few times you've been there since the breakup, they've flooded you with questions about your ex: "Hey, where is he/she today?" or "How is he/she doing?"

You have not been in the best of moods since the breakup, trying to heal it all and rebalance your life, and you haven't felt like telling the same old breakup story to everyone you met. So, when the annoying questions kept coming, all you said was: "He's fine," or "She is doing well, thanks."

Well, technically, you may not be lying. You may still hear about your ex, and from all accounts they are doing well. So, you may have been giving true information. You may have not been giving "all" the information you could have. And why should you? Your life is not anyone's business, right? You have the right to keep things to yourself! Yes!

Well, the thing though is that the questions keep coming and coming every time you go to those places. Most importantly though, when you go there, you can't help but think about the last time you and your ex were there together and what you did, what they did, what they said, what you said.

Frankly, those places just keep bringing the energy of the past to your mind, and that is something you know is not helping you move on. You also know that energetically, reminders of the old relationship and the feelings that those reminders bring up (pleasant or unpleasant) are taking up space where new energies need to come in.

In other words, in the weeks or months following a breakup, frequenting the old restaurants and shops that you and your ex spent a lot of time together in may not be good for the emotional healing that you need after a breakup, and consequently may not help you release the energies of the past. So, what do you do?

BREAK UP WITH THE RESTAURANT!

Yes. That's right. Until and unless you are ready to walk in there and say, "we are no longer together and I appreciate you not asking me about them anymore," it may be best to stay away for a while. How long is a while for you? Only you can answer that question, and the answer will be based on how much peace and closure you have given yourself about the breakup.

Note that I mentioned how much peace and closure YOU have given YOURSELF about the breakup. *The only person who can create inner peace inside you is you.* No matter what your ex can tell you about how sorry they are, no matter how much your friends and family tell you that the breakup was for your own good, only *you* can arrive at a place where your mind and heart are in agreement that the past needs to be released and that the breakup did not "damage" you. You must get to the place where you know, for sure, that the love you deserve and want will find its way to you. That is when you can fully release the old energies of the past.

You may seek the assistance of others to help get you to that emotional state, or you may be able to embody this mindset after doing some emotional healing on your own. Nevertheless, as I mentioned before, unless and until you are in a mental and emotional place where you truly can release the past with peace and still carry faith and hope for the future, it is perfectly OK (and even recommended) to avoid people, places, and things that bring you back to the energies of the past. That is, if you are not avoiding the world altogether. Remember to take care of your mental and emotional health, always.

> Please re-read the two paragraphs above as many times as you need to make sure you not only understand these concepts, but also know them in your bones and spirit. It is the essence of what we address in this book, and a recurring lesson throughout. Sure, it is a big lesson that takes time and lots of inner work, and that's why I've broken it down into different iterations in each of the book's eight chapters—to better clarify how that lesson manifests itself in the real world so that you can see how it applies to the different aspects of a breakup. Focus on this, and if you can understand this critical lesson, you will be in a great position to release old relationship energy and clear mental and emotional space for loving vibes to come into your life. This is my wish for you, and this is my intention with this book.

BREAKING UP WITH THE PLACES YOU AND YOUR EX FREQUENTLY VISITED

Well, the first option is not to go there. Forget about their yummy calamari! Or their delicious avocado toast (I sooooo love avocado toasts). If the restaurant still brings back memories of the old, just don't go. There are other places to eat, aren't there? Besides, it is not a forever boycott, remember? Just a temporary hiatus to give your heart time to let some memories go away.

Again, there is no glory in trying to appear strong. There is no need to "test" your emotional strength by forcing yourself to eat at a place where your heart is bleeding while your stomach is being satisfied. What if that restaurant, or café, or gym closed all of the sudden? Wouldn't you figure out a way to function without it? So, just imagine it closed and deal with it. Do not put yourself in situations or places that get you emotional on purpose. Don't do that to yourself. You have nothing to prove.

Now, if that calamari is so freaking delicious that you just cannot do without it, first ask yourself why you cannot detach from a food item. I may be making some jokes here, but when attachment to food or to anything gets to the point where it rules your life and you feel compelled to always pursue that thing, you may want to look into whether it is an issue that requires professional intervention or assistance.

Sometimes we shift our attachment (or obsession) from one thing we lost to another thing we still have access to. It is something to take seriously and may be a sign of behaviors or impulses we need to correct inside ourselves. Sometimes, the breakup itself may have happened to teach you NOT to be too attached to a person or to anything else, to the point where you feel you cannot live without it. So, if you find yourself obsessed with something after your breakup, please take a pause and examine your feelings and behaviors and see if it is a matter you need to address immediately and seriously.

Now, if you crave that calamari once in a while (like I do!) and you are one hundred percent sure that it is not because it reminds you of your ex, and it's not because you are trying to self-medicate with food, then you could try to see if the following options are available:

- ★ **Order in.** Yes, remember what you did during the pandemic? You ordered for delivery or takeout. That usually involves less interaction with people who may be the ones asking all the questions about your ex. The less talk about the past, the easier it is to release the energy of the past. Remember, what we focus on, or talk about, is what we attract into our lives.

★ **Find another restaurant that serves calamari.** Or another gym. Or another café. You get the idea, right? Find another place. You never know what a change in where you go can bring into your life. You may find that the food is better, the gym equipment is newer, the café serves better coffee, or you may meet people you would not have crossed paths with by going to the old places. If not, you still win by discovering new places and by spending less time thinking about old ones. Either way, it is good.

★ **Try different foods, take up hiking, or get a coffee maker at home.** Yes. What about trying something totally different? In an online 2020 article about breakups featured in *Psychology Today*, one post-breakup piece of advice given was to "fill your brain with new experiences."[5] Indeed, focusing on the new adventures as opposed to feeling bad about good old times is good for mental health overall. For example, do you know how much more benefit you get from hiking in nature versus only going to the gym? Now, gyms are good. However, everyone knows there's nothing like a run in the park, a hike around lakes and trees and fresh air. Ask yourself: "What need or want does that food or place satisfy for me"? Then look for other ways to get that same benefit and try it. You never know. Maybe you'll start loving hummus with pita chips and leave the calamari alone for a while. (Okay. Let's be honest, nothing can replace good calamari, ok… NOTHING! Well, for those who are into that food, like yours truly. However, I can tell you that a plate of hummus and pita chips hits the spot too, and it is often vegan…just saying.)

So, what is the moral of this story? Well, it is pretty much that you must forever boycott every place you went with your ex! *No, just kidding*. It doesn't have to be that drastic.

---

5 https://www.psychologytoday.com/us/blog/emotional-nourishment/201804/home-healing-space

However, please know that you do not need to force yourself to answer questions about your breakup until you are ready to do so, and you do not need to force yourself to frequent places that bring back memories you would rather forget. Releasing past energies sometimes requires stepping away for a while and changing your routine a bit. That is perfectly OK and that is a huge step towards self-love and self-healing. Prioritize healing your heart and clearing your energy, no matter what it takes. After doing the healing work, I promise, chances are that you could go to that restaurant and enjoy calamari again, okay? Have faith!

Why do you still watch your ex's IG if you really want to move on?

5 · Breaking Up with Old Pics, Social Media Posts, and Old Texts/Emails

Why are you still Facebook friends with your ex? And why are you stalking your ex's new person's Instagram? And you say you want to attract new love into your life? How is the new love going to come when you are swimming in the energy of the past, online? Would you want your new potential love interest to be doing the same? I didn't think so.

Let's talk about it.

To begin, let's get something out of the way quickly. We need to address the "I'm still friends with my ex" crowd. Yeah, that…

Not everyone is the same, and no relationships are the same. Not every breakup is horrible, bad, toxic, chaotic, violent, antagonistic, etc. Some exes can just agree to disagree and some even go farther and are able to remain friends after separating. We are not talking about cordial co-parenting here, which is an ideal to try to achieve because it is good for the children's mental health and overall wellbeing. That's good stuff right there, but that is not what I am focusing on here.

No. What I am referring to here is more than just being cordial and working together to maintain harmony and peace for the sake of the kids. I am talking about those who maintain friendships with their exes online and in person and stay active in each other's lives. We hear of exes going on vacation with each other's new family, maintaining one-on-one friendships, talking often, going out together, and so forth. For those who are able to do so without any old feelings of love, or anger, or sadness coming back up, I say: More power to y'all! Not everyone understands it, but if it works for you and contributes to your inner peace and self-love, then go for it.

Now, we *do* have to acknowledge the opinions of those who do not feel that such friendships are real or healthy. Again, I am not talking about parents keeping the peace for their children's sake. I am talking about the folks we mentioned above, staying connected on Facebook or Instagram, or even continuing as real-life close friends after a breakup.

WHY DO YOU WANT TO STAY INVOLVED?

Some say that those friendships are either a way to stay involved in an ex's life when one still carries a secret flame, or a way to still be in the mix and be able to have somewhat of an influence in your ex's new life. Others say such friendships are downright toxic, as the past should stay in the past and it is impossible to repress old feelings when in constant close proximity with a former lover. They warn of a slippery slope where accidents, aka "oops, we slept together," or "oops, the new wife fought with the old wife," are just waiting to happen.

To both of these perspectives, I say do not judge, but rather celebrate situations when peace and harmony exist between people who shared a part of their lives together. In other words, "Don't hate, appreciate." It is up to each person in a relationship to talk to the other about their comfort level with their partner being close to an ex. Whatever both sides agree on is what they should have the free will to do. To each their own.

But what if you do not agree with the notion of staying close to an ex, for whatever reason. In that case I ask again, if you and your ex do not remain friends in the real world, why are you social media friends? Well, unless you are in the group of people who found an honest/safe way to stay close to their former mates after a breakup, then you must break up with their social media, pictures, texts, emails, and other digital connections!

The following are a few things to consider in this matter.

What is the need that is fulfilled in you when you watch their social media? Do you stay Facebook friends because you care about how your ex is doing? Is your interest related to their wellbeing? Why do you feel you need to know that information? If you are divorced, you may say that you want to know if they are acting properly because your kids sometimes stay with your ex. However, the vast majority of divorced couples or separated couples who have children together manage to assess that without snooping on their former partners via social media.

> If you feel you have concerns about your kids' safety, please go to legal professionals or the authorities to determine how to proceed. This book is not advice on how to handle such issues.

Also consider why you feel you need to know what your ex is doing with their life? Could it be one or more of the reasons below?

★ You are nosy and want to know if your ex is happy without you.
★ You want to know if your ex's new person is better looking than you.
★ You want to know if your ex is miserable or happy (and you prefer the former).
★ You want to know if they are doing what you wish they had done while you guys were together.
★ You want to emulate what his new person is doing so they don't seem better than you.
★ You want your ex to see your profile to see what they are missing.
★ You sincerely want to know how your ex is doing.

You know the common theme that runs through those options? YOU STILL CARE! In other words, you still carry your ex's energy in your heart, mind, and spirit. In an article published online on the website, *Power of Positivity*, psychologist Yvonne Thomas, Ph.D., is quoted saying: "From a mental health perspective, you shouldn't keep tabs on your ex on social media because you can't have a genuine, clean break and really move forward while you are staying in your ex's life even if it is remotely through social media… Social media stalking is like taking the scab off the wound that's starting to heal from the breakup and then having to start the healing process all over again."[6]

---

6 https://www.powerofpositivity.com/why-you-shouldnt-talk-to-ex-social-media/

Now, let me ask you: How is keeping tabs on your ex through social media helping you move on? Why do you still care? And if you care because you are still in love with them, or because you are still mad at them, how is virtually stalking them going to help you move on?

IT'S TIME TO RELEASE THOSE ENERGETIC ATTACHMENTS ON SOCIAL MEDIA

It is hard to let go of someone you love who you truly feel is your "other half." (That is, *figuratively speaking*, because we are whole on our own). I know it is not easy. Many of us have been there. However, holding on to love that is not reciprocated does not help bring anyone back to you. If someone is really meant for you, detaching from them and focusing on your own self-love is the way to attract new love to you. And if you do that and the old love doesn't come back, trust that something better is heading your way.

True love does not make the other person wait. There may be times when separation is needed to reinforce real love and help people appreciate their partners better, but it is usually not the type of separation in which there is total ghosting and total abandonment.

Breaking up with your ex's social media is one way to release energetic attachment to the past, and so is deleting old pics from your phone or old emails. If you need to keep certain documents for legal or financial purposes, then of course do so. However, having old pics on your phone may make it more difficult to look towards the present and the future. Also, think about this: Would you like to see pictures of old girlfriends or boyfriends on the phone or social media of the new person entering your love life? You must be willing to do for others what you are asking/expecting others to do for you.

So, the moral of this social media story is this: Let it go. Turn it off, block, delete, erase. Break up with it. There may be a day where you are able to reconnect with your ex, but at least in the beginning, give your heart a chance to focus on you and to have some peace. Your heart deserves that, right?

Did someone say sexual detox? Hmmm... Yup!

6 · Breaking Up with Old Energies of Intimacy

(Yes, press pause on the "dancy dance,"
if you know what I mean.)

Okay. Yup. We are going THERE! Down there, or all up in there. Take it however you like.

Anyway, yes, you read the title right. It may be time to BREAK UP with the remnants of sexual energy from past relationships that may still linger in your own energy, and even in your body, some say. There are countless books, articles, and talks out there which all go into how our physical and emotional bodies carry what they call "energetic residue" from past sexual relationships, and that this residue can carry energy that can be either damaging or healing, depending on the nature of the former relationship.

Indeed, from sexual energy cleansing toolkits available for sale everywhere, to *limpiezas* done in many Latin and Caribbean cultures, to sexual energy cleansing baths using herbs, fruits, and minerals in other parts of the world (we're not talking about showering together here), there are many variations of sexual cleansing practices that are highly encouraged after leaving a relationship, as a means to release old energy and prepare energetic space for new, loving energies to come in.

Some Indian cultures, for example, believe that sexual recalibration can be done through the process of Kundalini awakening, in which divine feminine energy starts moving from the base of the spine to the top of the head, resulting in energy clearing and strengthening of the body and the nervous system. Some say that following the process for Kundalini activation while abstaining from sex allows that "kundalini fuel" or internal fire to recycle internally and heal any sexual blockage or energetic attachment to old sexual partners. It cleans the energy of the person following the kundalini awakening process, as opposed to passing that healing energy to another person through sex. In other words, one can heal one's own sexual energy by generating that energy for oneself, and letting that sexual energy remain on the inside to heal the body and the heart from the inside, out.

In plain English, what this means is that there are many who believe that one should have a "pause" in between sexual partners to ensure the energy from the old is fully released from the body, mind, and spirit. This can be achieved through the methods described above and through a multitude of other ways, including self-healing with temporary abstinence, herbal baths or teas, meditation, mindful breathing, and energy healing with the assistance of spiritual healers, reiki, prayer, diet, eating clean foods, fasting, and other practices.

THE MANY PATHWAYS OF SEXUAL DETOX

Many of those rituals or processes may seem like they apply to women, and many in fact do, as there is a belief among some that women absorb energy from their partners in a deeper and longer lasting way. However, sexual detox can be done by men in many of the ways mentioned earlier, including taking a break and not having sex for a little while. We know many men may say that is an impossible feat, and an unrealistic expectation, but many others would agree that they can summon enough courage and self-control to take time off and allow their bodies to release past energies from old partners. We can just say this to the men: When you find that queen who respects herself and values the energy they carry, they will give you many points for being able to value yourself enough to take that sexual break after a breakup. So, just keep your friend in for a little while, ok?

Some may find this section amusing, and it can be quite a funny topic, but it is a serious matter. Many more folks will understand its importance and value. In this book, we just lay out ideas and factors for you to consider in making sure your energy is as clear and love-attracting as possible. The choice to put some of our suggestions into practice, or not to do so, is totally and completely yours. No judgment here.

In case you are thinking of what to do with all your own energy during this sexual pause, there are a few ways to release some steam and feel active:

- ★ **Work out at home or at the gym.** Exercise is a good way to relieve stress and improve your body. Always consult your healthcare professional before doing any physical activity. Exercise doesn't have to be two hours of cardio or weightlifting. It can consist of a walk, a jog, moving around at home, or even dancing. Whatever you are capable of doing and whatever makes you happy.
- ★ **Try gardening.** Although it may be a breeze for some, most gardening involves moving around, bending, stretching, digging—all types of activity that can give you that tired-but-satisfied feeling of effort well expended. It is a good way to use available physical energy.
- ★ **Meditate.** Although not necessarily a sweat-producing physical activity, meditation calls for focus, concentration, and discipline, all of which can use up some of the available energy, both mental and physical.

There is always that other option which involves taking matters into your own hands, if you know what I mean, for those who feel it is a choice that should be on the table too. Whether or not that is your thing, you do what you feel is best for you. No judgment here.

So, the moral of this section? Zip it, lock it, hide it, send it on hiatus, put it away—but give your body a break. Take time to breathe out, wash out, cleanse out the old energies, and breathe in new, healing, loving vibes. Be mindful as you go through this period of what you wish to achieve with this pause and ask your body to help you do the release. It listens and it wants to help you because it loves you. So, love it right back by giving it a break. Okay love? Can you do that? Sure you can, because you love yourself and because a little self-control is not too much to ask.

*Why are you still upset about your breakup?
Is it because you still care?*

7 · Breaking Up with Resentment and Regret (Do It for You)

If you ask a hundred people who have had an unsatisfactory first date, one of the most common reasons for the disappointment is that the other person spent most of the date talking about their ex and how the ex was horrible or crazy.

Have you experienced that? If you have, please trust me when I say, you are not alone in this. People complaining about exes on a first date is one of the most popular reasons for many "thank-you-but-no-second-date" outcomes.

Who wants to spend an entire evening listening to someone else ranting about the woes of their past relationship? When you hear that, what is the first thing that comes to your mind? Here are some questions you may imagine asking your date when in that situation:

★ Are you over your ex?
★ Why do you still care?
★ Why are you still angry?
★ Was the problem you?
★ Do you even see me sitting across the table from you?
★ Do you even care about who I am and what I am looking for?
★ Are you one of those serial killers we hear about in the news?

Okay, just kidding about the last question. However, listening to stories about someone's old flame does nothing to give you confidence that you are dealing with a person who is emotionally stable, and more importantly, somebody READY to get into a new relationship.

But what if the person complaining is you? That is what we want to assess here, and that is what you want to understand. And you know why? Because these types of thoughts keep old attachments in your own energy and may block you from truly moving on.

So, when it comes to feelings of resentment, anger, sadness, and regret towards your ex, what do you do? BREAK UP WITH THEM ALL!

> Just as a little reminder before I dive deep into this section, I want to once again emphasize a very important point: An energetic separation from your ex is just as important, if not more important, than a physical separation, and it should be done after every breakup to allow energetic room for new love to come into your life.
> That said, it is not rocket science to understand that holding on to feelings of anger and resentment towards your ex just keeps you attached to them. It's common sense. Period.

Consider what feelings of resentment or anger may say about your emotional state, and a few steps you can take to make them go away:

★ **You still feel betrayed and mistreated.** That, unfortunately, is something that comes after many breakups. Someone cheated, did not keep their promises, outright lied, pretended they were someone they were not, stole money from you, sabotaged finances, etc. While you may be justified in feeling those emotions, you also have to realize that they do not help in healing your heart. Emotions must be given the chance to rise, be acknowledged, be present, and then healed or alchemized into fuel to empower you and make you wiser. Emotions are not to be suppressed or ignored, for they are a message from your inner self to your consciousness saying that something needs to be addressed.

★ **You feel you need to get justice for what happened to you.** In other words, you want your ex to pay a price for the breakdown of the relationship, if you feel you were not the problem. Once again, this is a common feeling among those who've dealt with this situation. Sometimes it seems like life is not fair and that one party got the short end of the stick. Although that may seem like it is the case, feeling robbed by life or feeling taken advantage of does not promote emotional healing and energetic detachment from old relationships.

★ **You are mad at yourself for not seeing that the relationship would end up in a breakup, and perhaps a bad breakup.** This is something people experience a lot after separation, and it is not a good feeling. Self-blame sometimes acts as a cover for the embarrassment one feels once the relationship is over and issues that were not given much attention start resurfacing after a reexamination of the facts of the relationship. This is where people go: "Oh, I should have seen it coming," or "this was a clue about their character that I ignored," or "how could I have believed his story about working late every day that week?" Self-blame can result in building up anger that ends up being directed at those you interact with whether you are aware of it or not.

ACKNOWLEDGING YOUR FEELINGS

Why is it important to acknowledge the feelings described above and what does that have to do with clearing past relationship energies from your life? I'll explain.

Whether you feel love or hate towards someone, it means that you have an energetic attachment to them. And when you have energetic attachment to people, it is akin to a form of power in your life and even power over you. In other words, when you have feelings for people, whether they are loving or ill-intended feelings, it is like you give them a string attached to your heart that they have the power to pull when they so wish. Often, when the feeling is love, you don't see it as a threat, as you most likely expect love in return, as with friends and family and loved ones.

However, when the feeling is one of hate or anger or resentment, you put your emotional body at the mercy of people who do not have any loving intentions towards you, thus opening the door to getting hurt over and over. What many don't grasp, when it comes to resenting someone, is that the person feeling the resentment is the one giving the power to the person they resent. If we flip that over, we can see that the reverse is true as well, in that when we stop resenting people, we take away their power to have a hold on our emotions.

Does that mean that people you don't care about can't hurt you? No, that is not what we are saying here. What we are saying is that the more you reduce your emotional attachment to people, the less power they have to upset you. You are human and have a heart, and as such, feeling hurt by someone will always be a possibility. However, the more inner peace and emotional strength you carry, the less you are frazzled by what others or life throws your way.

When we talk of energetically clearing old disempowering energies, we focus on doing our best to maintain an atmosphere of inner peace, joy, confidence, and hope, in our hearts, minds, and spirits. Breaking up with the things we discuss in this book is a proven way of clearing up energetic space around us, and the impact of that clearing is that we make space for loving and empowering energies to come and stay in our lives. That is the point of what we are doing here.

So, what do you do if you are still harboring those feelings towards your breakup?

IF THE PAIN CONTINUES

If you are still feeling upset about your breakup long after it happens, then it may be a good idea to consider getting some mental health assistance, whether it is by going within and doing some healing work, or by enlisting the help of a professional. No matter what you feel someone did "to" you, at the end of the day, that person did it "for" themselves, for whatever reason. It may seem unfair, but again, people have free will and the right to follow what they feel is in their best interest, even if they do it with the intention to purposely hurt you.

Emotional healing and inner work are not easy and take time, so don't be too hard on yourself. It is okay to hold your ex accountable for their mistreatment of you, but your main focus, your long-term focus, needs to stay on your own healing and any lessons you can learn about yourself from the breakup.

Again, no matter what others may feel they are doing to you, it is the story you tell yourself about what your breakup meant to you that matters. Saying "I was betrayed" versus, "I went through an experience that is teaching me to be more discerning in choosing my partners" makes a huge difference. The first statement can make you feel powerless, while the second statement puts the power to change back in your hands, and thus, changes the entire energy around you from low to high.

I've covered emotional healing in my first book, *An Apology to My Demons*. Emotional healing often takes one back to childhood experiences in which a situation may have created a disempowering self-belief that needs to be dismantled by doing some inner child healing work. Therefore, it is not a topic I can cover here in a quick manner. So, please feel free to refer to my first book in your emotional healing journey, especially to understand some of the underlying emotional issues that may have come up during the course of your old relationship.

What many people don't know is that relationships are where many childhood traumas or other emotional wounds come up for healing. It is where they get an opportunity to be acknowledged and cleared away. That is why many say that many so-called "daddy issues" resurface in relationships with one's husband or one's sons, and many so-called "mommy issues" resurface in relationships with one's wife or daughters.

If we, as a society, spread this message more and prepare couples to be ready for that as they navigate relationships, I believe many problems couples face would be treated differently. While partners would still communicate with each other about how they feel the other could do better in the relationship, they would also understand that the issues they face may be a reflection of something internal that they need to address for themselves. It would lead to more introspection, self-reflection, and accountability, and put less pressure on trying to have the other partner assume the pressure of having to fix everything by him/herself.

RELEASING OLD ENERGIES, WHETHER TOXIC OR NOT

If you ask: "But what if the breakup was amicable? Would you still have old energies to release?" The answer is yes. You may feel, since the energy of that past was never toxic or negative, you may not need to get rid of relationship-related people, places, and things in the same way as someone who had a bad experience, right? Well, actually, the answer is a complex one. Let's talk about it.

When breakups occur in a friendly fashion with no hard feelings, it sometimes is harder to remove the energy of the old relationship because it is not believed to pose any threat to emotional health. Indeed, many see it as a sign of maturity and great emotional intelligence when two people are able to part ways on good terms. However, this type of separation may require even more effort to clear energetic attachment than breakups that happened in a hostile way.

The reason for this is that in cordial separations, there often remain positive (maybe even loving) feelings towards the other person that may easily blur the lines of friendship after a few glasses of wine. In such amicable separations, couples tend to remain friends and end up staying in the same circles, thus are easily able to keep in touch with each other. That means they stay in each other's energy fields. This sometimes creates blockages for new romantic relationships to come into their lives because it may send the signal to the Universe that the partners may still be interested in each other in a deeper way.

So, what is the bottom line in all of this? Whether you feel anger towards your ex or a little bit of love for them, it is a good idea to detach completely, at least at first, to allow the emotions to stabilize and signal to the Universe that your wish is to move on with new beginnings and new energies.

Are you still grieving the fiftieth wedding anniversary party that will never happen?

8 · Breaking Up with Old Dreams, Plans, and Wishes

(Use an alternate ending for your life movie.)

Breaking up your romantic visions of the future is a hard one, but with a good perspective you can not only heal from unfulfilled dreams, but also allow much better ones to be realized in your life.

When relationships reach the point of being seen as long-term and committed, couples make plans together for years to come. Some even make concrete decisions with work and career and location of residence, based on the idea that their relationship will last their whole lives and that they will always have their partners by their sides. Those big life-changing decisions are seldom made lightly and usually involve a road map planned long into the future, for decades to come.

Indeed, from the time two people seemingly become serious and start talking about being together forever, they may start making dreams of how they would spend their golden years in houses full of grandkids, or perhaps making a family of just two and traveling around the world for decades to come. Those dreams affect decisions in the current moment, and some of those decisions cannot be undone.

This is why, when a breakup occurs, having to part with long-term dreams can be so hard to deal with and so difficult to process. In fact, it can be devastating beyond what can be seen or understood in the current moments. It is even harder for people who have made drastic changes in their lives to be with their partners, such as moving to a new country, having kids, getting a pet, and other joint endeavors.

There are those who unfortunately don't understand this and who feel like the only thing that is lost from a failed relationship is time as it relates to the number of weeks/months/years couples spent together. You often hear people say such things as: "Well, thank God you only wasted two years of your life with your ex." They completely miss the impact that breakups can have on people's plans for their future. Separation often causes ex-partners to have to forgo dreams and goals that were made when the relationship was going well.

Just a quick note for anyone who feels like a failed partnership is a waste of time. Time spent working in good faith on a relationship, or on anything in life for that matter, is never a waste. Good karma is always created for those whose hearts were in the right place. Furthermore, any experience in life carries with it lessons and wisdom, which can be used to foster discernment, which is a helpful tool in making important decisions in life. As my podcast title states, the goal in life is to "alchemize it all," and turn all of our lemons into lemonade.

CONSIDERING AN ALTERNATE ENDING

To be completely vulnerable with you, one of my dreams was celebrating fifty years of marriage with someone, as I saw my grandparents do. I remember thinking during their golden anniversary celebration that I also wanted that for me one day. Even after my divorce, I still felt young enough to have that fifty-year celebration with someone, even if it was not for marriage. I also was okay with something like forty years of marriage, but fifty years together. Now, at my age, it is still doable since it would just mean I'd have to live into my mid-nineties (and so would my would-be life partner if they and I were around the same age) but the possibility of that happening obviously gets slimmer as time passes by.

For a few years of my life, it made me really sad that I may not get that celebration. It almost felt like I failed my grandparents by not being able to replicate their example. It also felt like I let myself down, as I blamed myself for years for not taking the right decisions or making the right choices in my love life. Now I feel differently: more hopeful, more confident, and more joyful than ever. And the reason for this is a term I've grown to love thanks to a YouTube video I saw about a movie

I once saw, *The Notebook*. The term in question was the title of the video: "Alternate Ending."

(Spoiler alert: Please skip this paragraph if you plan to see the film.) One day I was watching clips of that movie and came across a video in which the protagonist Ally ended up marrying Lon, her fiancé. It showed Ally going back to Lon after spending time with her first love, Noah, and Ally deciding to continue with her planned wedding and become Lon's wife. In the original ending, Ally had canceled her wedding and had gone back to be with Noah. When I saw the video, I immediately understood why the universe had pulled me to look into clips of the movie that morning. One of the side effects of emotional healing, as I discuss in my first book, has been an incredible spiritual awakening for me, which has made me more discerning when it comes to divine messages about how to heal my heart. I am grateful to the Universe for that ability and that shift in my perspective on life and life events.

I knew, after seeing the last video clip, that the point of that experience for me was the message of the video, as my attention kept going back to the title, "Alternate Ending." I barely remember what the characters said in the clip, for my focus stayed on those two words. Soon enough my mind started to wonder why. As I pondered that question, I realized what this term came into my reality to teach me: *When things change after you've had a preplanned ending in your mind, don't worry. Just create an alternate ending that fills you with joy, hope, and gratitude.* And that is what I did in many areas of my life.

Imagining your alternate ending

How do you use the concept of "alternate ending" to release the energy of old relationship dreams that will never come to pass?

One of the amazing abilities human beings have is the ability to imagine. To see scenarios, objects, conclusions, situations, and anything else we want, inside our minds. Another great ability people have is to be able to articulate the things they imagine and take steps to bring them to life. When we use the word "ability," others may even say that imagination is a "superpower" humans possess, as everything we see in the real world started in someone's imagination or in the imagination of the Universe/God/Creator, however you refer to that energy/force.

That imagination allows you to create an alternate ending when life takes a turn that you did not expect, and you feel forced to go back to the drawing board. As noted earlier, it is not easy to say goodbye to old dreams. I understand. But think about this: What new dreams can you now create from where your life is right now? What can be an amazing, delicious, joyful, exciting alternate ending for your story?

Following are some things to consider as you rewrite your dreams for your life, for your new beginning. (Note that I said, "new beginning," not new ending. Do you know why? Well, I stated that because every ending is just the other side of a new beginning, and vice versa.)

Having new dreams does not mean you give up on things that make you happy.

If you had dreamed of retiring in St. Croix with your former fiancé and now you have broken up, having new dreams does not mean you give up on your retirement plans. It just means that you start imagining yourself there with someone you love. When you think about it, don't focus on the features and name of your partner, but the feeling you would feel when you are in their arms, dancing by the beach. Close your eyes and feel happy and tell yourself, "I am so happy I get to retire here with the love of my life."

It is okay to change some dreams.

When you got together with your ex, you definitely were *younger,* and you may have been relatively inexperienced about life, work, and the world in general. So, were your old dreams based on an old version of you? Now that you have a chance to dream some new dreams, do your old dreams still fit who you are today?

Here's one example. Let's say that before your relationship, you had never traveled the world. One of the vacations you took with your ex was to a Pacific Island where you found a place where they find work for women who escaped domestic violence. Since that first trip, you've traveled there every two years and have established a great relationship with the organization. It's almost like you found your calling by associating with the women, as it fills your heart with so much joy to see them rebuilding their lives.

Before your breakup, you may not have done all you wanted to do with that organization because you had established certain dreams that would not allow you to go all out with supporting the causes of those women. However, now that you are taking time to create new dreams, you may decide to become a spokesperson for them and open a little non-profit here at home to spread the word and support them in a bigger way. Do you see what I mean by changing your dreams a bit? Who knows where that could take you, but more importantly, who knows how much more joy it could bring into your life?

Remember, as I have stated many times in this book, *filling your heart with happy and joyful energies is one of the main ways to push out disempowering past energies.* By doing something you love in a bigger way, you force your mind to focus on that, thus leaving it little time to focus on issues and people of the past. It is also a way to make room for new loving energies to come into your life, as good energy attracts good energy.

Replace old dreams with what really matters.

So, yes, I may have to say goodbye to my dreams of celebrating fifty years of marriage to someone, though there is still time for me to do so. However, any time spent with someone you really love and who loves you back is worth celebrating. So, I don't put too much energy into that dream now, and just focus on being joyful and grateful in the present moment.

Instead of being a "must-do or it's a failure," that dream is now more like a "would-be-nice" thing. My new dream now is to have beautiful adventures, amazing stories, and live a purposeful life. It is happening, and I feel gratitude for it in my heart. As for how many years I'll spend with my special person, I wish we stay together for a very long time, but I no longer put a specific time frame on it. I leave that up to the Universe. I surrender to life, knowing that the Universe wants me to be happy, content, and grateful. In the meantime, I focus on fulfilling my life's purpose, and being the best human I can be, while learning and growing every day.

I hope you feel it is okay to say goodbye to some dreams too if you feel you must. However, don't forget that goodbye to one dream means hello to another. So, what dreams are you saying hello to today?

One last breakup: Break up with the "need" to find love again.

Okay Universe! I'm Ready (for New Beginnings) Whenever You Are!

Just do your best, follow your bliss,
and let life take care of the rest.

Now that you have broken up with many things that kept you energetically tied to the past, I must mention one last one, and it is by far the most important and consequential breakup of your life: Breaking up with the idea of "needing" someone in your life to be happy and fulfilled.

I know, I know. How do you stop wanting to find someone to share your life with? Isn't that what most people want?

I hear you, but please hear me out.

If you very carefully read what I stated above, you will see that I am talking about letting go of the mindset that you cannot be happy on your own. That does not mean you cannot hope and dream of having a special someone in your life. All it means is that you KNOW, for sure, that you can find happiness and joy in many ways, and that you will not "ignore" or "undervalue" other paths to happiness while waiting for your life partner to connect with you.

What that looks like in real life is that *you pursue what makes you happy, every day, with what you currently have in the present moment.* As you continue to allow your heart to expand and find more things that bring you joy, you try your best to live in gratitude and say a word of thanks for those things.

What it looks like is you releasing the need to please others and to be accepted, and doing what makes your heart smile.

It's releasing judgment towards those who do not let their hearts lead the way like you do and not condemning or criticizing them. It is allowing them to be. Free will, remember?

It's always keeping space in your life for your special person to come in when the time is right, and not being so busy that other loving energies can't find a way through to you.

It's forgiving yourself and forgiving others, but not allowing everyone back in since guarding your inner peace is now your main priority.

It's getting back up when you make a mistake or when life sends you another lesson, and still having faith that life loves you.

It's understanding that all is well, all the time, even when it doesn't feel like it, or look like it.

It's a lot more things, more than I can enumerate in this book alone, but you get the point. Keep believing in love, knowing that love starts within and towards yourself first. And keep believing that you deserve the life of your dreams, as you keep forging ahead and taking inspired action towards achieving your goals.

Many say that in order to really cleanse your mind, heart, and spirit from past energies, you have to wish your exes well and send them love energetically. If you wish to do that, go ahead. However, in this book, getting to a mental and emotional space where you can make "peace" with the breakup and understand the lessons it brought for your own growth and expansion is the ultimate goal.

When you understand that the breakup was not about the person you were with, but it was a tool that the Universe used to enlighten you, teach you, help you grow and be more empowered, then the person you broke up with becomes somewhat irrelevant. You feel no ill feelings towards them and do not force yourself to continuously send good vibes to them either. Their energy just disappears as you feel gratitude for the person you are today, and you feel excitement about the person you are becoming day by day. Isn't that thought alone deliciously intoxicating?

And finally...

8 *More* Little Bites of Wisdom as You Start a Deliciously Amazing New Chapter of Your Life

1. You deserve to feel love and to be loved.
2. There are things in life you cannot control and that's okay. Don't fight them. Surrender.
3. People have free will. They do things "for" themselves and not "to" you. Let them be.
4. You can create New Dreams and Alternate Endings for your life any time you wish to do so.
5. True love begins from yourself to yourself. If/when you find it in others, it's only a beautiful bonus.
6. Life wants you to succeed and be happy. It is on your side. Trust your journey.
7. The Universe does not punish. It only teaches. Find the lessons and release the hurts.
8. Walk with purpose, walk with gratitude, walk with faith, and walk with love… and all will work out for you, somehow, always.

I wish you love, I wish you peace, I wish you joy, and lots and lots of deliciousness.

Love, always,
Mama Bear

Epilogue

Her: "Hello!"

Company: "Yes, may we help you?"

Her: "I'm here to rent a moving van."

Company: "Will you be driving it?"

Her: "Yes. I'm donating a lot of items I own because I am moving to my new, amazing, country home with my loved ones, and our dogs, our chickens, and our horses. I will be living closer to my children and be in an area I love. We hired a moving company for the house move. However, I just need a van for the items I am happily donating to Goodwill."

Company: "What's your name?"

Her: "My name is…"

Company: "You're in our system. You rented a van from us a few years ago."

Her: "Yes. I remember."

Company: "It must have been a good experience since you came back to us."

Her: "It didn't seem like a good thing at first, but over time, I understood that it was one of the best moves of my life and one of the Universe's biggest blessings for me… and for that, I am grateful."

…And she, her loved ones, and their dogs, horses, and chickens, are all living happily ever after.

The End (well, the beginning)…

Resources for Mental and Emotional Health

It is not weak to ask for help. Getting yourself the support you need is an act of courage, self-love and self-care. You are not alone. There are many ways to get help. If you or someone you know need assistance with mental/emotional health issues, contact one or more of the following associations and government agencies:

- ★ The Anxiety and Depression Association of America: https://adaa.org/find-help
- ★ Emergency Medical Services: 911
- ★ Mental Health America: https://www.mhanational.org/finding-help
- ★ MentalHealth.gov
- ★ https://www.mentalhealth.gov/get-help/immediate-help
- ★ https://www.mentalhealth.gov/what-to-look-for
- ★ https://www.mentalhealth.gov/get-help
- ★ National Suicide Prevention Lifeline: 1-800-273-TALK (8255) or https://suicidepreventionlifeline.org/
- ★ National Alliance on Mental Illness: https://www.nami.org/Home
- ★ The National Child Traumatic Stress Network: https://www.nctsn.org/resources
- ★ Substance Abuse and Mental Health Services Administration (SAMHSA) Treatment Referral Helpline: 1-877-SAMHSA7 (726-4727)

Index

air, fresh, 16, 23
alternate endings, 52–56, 59
amicable breakups, 50
anger, at self, 47
  apartment
  airing out, 23
  breaking up with, 19–26
  cleansing, 22–23
  decorating, 20, 22, 24–25
  imagining new, 21–22
  moving from, 20–21
  painting, 25
  purging old energy from, 22–23
Apology to My Demons, An (Katherine), 49
attachment, problematic, 34

belongings
  airing out, 16
  breaking up with, 9–17
  changing story of, 16–17
  cleansing, 15–16
  donating/selling, 13–14
  energy in, 9–11
  expense of replacing, 12
  harder/larger items, 13–17
  questions to ask regarding, 14–15
  reasons for keeping, 12–13
betrayal, feelings of, 46, 49

blame
  avoiding, 23
  of self, 47
blessings, 26
breakups, experiences of, vii–viii, 1–2

Carmichael, Chloe, 20
cars, cleansing, 26
childhood traumas, 49
children, 10, 39
Chopra, Deepak, 30
cleansing, 15–16, 22–23
clothing, 10–11

decorating, 20, 22, 24–25
detaching energetically, importance of, 4–6
digital connections, 37–40
dreams
  breaking up with, 51–56
  creating new, 59
Dyer, Wayne, 16

Einstein, Albert, 4
emails, deleting, 40
endings, alternate, 52–56, 59
energetic detachment, 6
energetic signatures, 5

energy
  avoiding negative, 23
  in belongings, 9–11
  following focus, 4
  impact of, 4
  purging old, 22–23
  research on, 5
  sexual, 41–43
exercise, 43
exes
  complaining about, 45–46
  energy of, 4
  memories of, vi–vii
  remaining friends with, 37–38
  reminders of, 2–3
expense of replacing items, 12

family and friends
  by association, 27–28
  breaking up with, 27–30
  holding off on contacting, 28–29
feelings, acknowledging, 47–48
focus, energy following, 4
free will, 29, 38, 48–49, 57, 59
fresh air, 16, 23
furniture, moving, 24
future, changing plans for, 51–56

gardening, 43

house
  airing out, 23
  breaking up with, 19–26
  cleansing, 22–23
  decorating, 20, 22, 24–25
  imagining new, 21–22
  moving from, 20–21
  painting, 25
  purging old energy from, 22–23

imagination, 53–54
inner child healing work, 49
intimacy, old energies of, 41–43

jealousy, 13, 14
justice, feeling need for, 46–47

Kundalini awakening, 41–42

limpiezas, 41
Lipton, Bruce, 5
low vibrational states/feelings, 7

mattresses, replacing, 24
meditation, 43
mental health assistance, 48
mindset, shifting, 16–17
moving, 20–21. see also house

negative energy, avoiding, 23
new experiences, 35
new love
  barriers to, 21
  readiness for, 57–58
  self-love and, 40
Notebook, The, 53

offices, cleansing, 26

painting, 25
pictures, deleting, 40
places, breaking up with, 31–36
plans, breaking up with, 51–56
purging old energy, 22–23

questions, responding to, 31–32, 36

resentment and regret, breaking up with, 45–50
restaurants, 31, 32, 34–35
ride-or-die friends, 27–28
Robbins, Tony, 4

saging, 15, 22–23, 26
self-blame, 47
sexual detox, 42–43
sexual energy, 41–43
sheets, new, 24
social media, breaking up with, 37–40
stories, changing, 16–17
strength, 6–7, 12
stress, 7, 43

Thomas, Yvonne, 39
Travers, James, 11

www.ingramcontent.com/pod-product-compliance
Lightning Source LLC
Chambersburg PA
CBHW070102100426
42743CB00012B/2631